Ask A Silly

CW00572121

Messages fr
trickiest c

Fredrick Facedass

for my beautiful Michelle

Acknowledgements

Huge thanks to Andrew Lownie, Jo Cantello and David Haviland for their unrivalled ability to spot a great book, their superb sense of humour and for allowing me to (very crudely) blow my own trumpet in their acknowledgement.

Further (but equally huge) thanks must go to my parents, Michelle Davies, Joseph Glavey, James Glavey, Katie Pickwoad, Matt Robins and all those who have been kind enough to give me a quote.

A special mention must go to everyone who bothered replying to Fredrick- you are a testament to the (almost) limitless patience and goodwill of mankind.

Anyone else who feels I should be thankful to them- I am thankful, just more forgetful.

All the correspondence in this book is completely genuine.
Usernames have been changed to protect real identities.

Improve your memory
a personal spell cast by a green witch

Quantity: **9 available**

Price: **£9.99**   Buy it now

Seller info
cornishwitch (745)   Item location: Cornwall
100% Positive Feedback

This is a powerful Wiccan Magick personal spell that will improve memory for the recipient

In times of stress or when you are tired or even in the later years it sometimes dawns upon you that your memory is not quite up to par. This spell will help you...

From: redfacedass
To: cornishwitch

Dear Cornishwitch,

Hope you are well.

TALIA (wife)(mine)-
"We have got everything we need, except for tinned tomatoes and some fresh coriander. Can you pick some up on the way home from work please darling?"

FREDRICK (me)-
"No problem. See you soon."

I returned to a very unhappy wife with some seeded grapes (I hate seeded grapes), one cabbage and some scampi flavoured Nik Naks. This is just today's example. Yesterday I forgot her birthday…

You see Cornishwitch, I have struggled with my memory for as long as I can remember.
The situation has become so desperate that I'm worried I may lose my job, my wife or worse still myself.

I have tried everything- except witchcraft…

Do you think you could help me?

I would be forever grateful.
Fredrick Facedass

From: cornishwitch

To: redfacedass

Merry meet Fredrick!

Thank you for your question about my personal spell cast. I understand completely as I have always had to manage a poor memory personally. A good memory is not a natural attribute of mine and I find that the busier I am the more stressed out and the more things that I have to juggle, some things just slip the net. However, if it's affecting your work and your relationship, this isn't good and of course I can help.

I'll need you to click on the 'buy it now' button on my shop and pay me through PayPal-then send me all the following details about yourself-

Full name
DOB
Detailed physical description or photo
Favourite food
Favourite drink
What you do for a living
Details of your family arrangements
How long you have been married
How you met, if you have children or pets, their names and ages- seriously!

I know it sounds like loads, but it helps me to link with you on a personal level so that I can make the spell very powerful and lasting for you.

I am available to cast this very night for you and as it was my birthday only yesterday, I am most powerful at this time of year. I believe that people's paths cross for a reason just as we need each other the most.

I'm so pleased that you found me, as I know I can help you with this as I have helped so many before.

Love and my
Brightest blessings,

Maria x

From: redfacedass
To: cornishwitch

Name- Fredrick Frascuelo Facedass

DOB- May 19th 1973 Nicosia (Cyprus)

Detailed physical description-
I have a golden sheen to my white skin.

My dimensions are: 6ft (height) / 40in (chest) / 34in (waist) / 2.5-5.5in (penis) / and size 10 (shoe).

I would either describe my body as average or athletic depending on whether I was trying to impress.

I am often complemented on my hands- I am blessed with fine cuticles.

I have a very aggressive head of dark hair with no signs of balding or receding. I have no beard, but could certainly achieve this if I desired.

I am rather handsome. I have big brown eyes.

One potentially useful (Not sure how this all works?) fact about myself is that I have breast tissue forming in my chest. Not even my wife knows this (I DO TRUST THIS REMAINS CONFIDENTIAL).

Favourite food- 'Stifado'- a Cypriot stew (cooked by mama). Seedless grapes (I hate seeded grapes) and Nik Naks.

Favourite drink- Apple flavoured Lucozade.

What you do for a living- Taxi driver.

Details of your family arrangements- I have arranged with my father never ever to see him again. I recently arranged for my grandparents ashes to be sprinkled across the Pedieos, the longest river in Cyprus (the place my mother and I were both conceived and also the place where my father tried to drown me and my brother Tulio).

How long you have been married- I have been married to Talia for almost 10 years (I think?).

How you met- Talia rescued my brother (Tulio) and I from the river Pedieos.

Children or pets- I have a dog named Stephen who is 4 months old.

From: redfacedass
To: cornishwitch

Dear Maria,

How are you? I'm OK, thanks.

Did everything go well with the spell that you cast for me? I only ask because my memory has been pretty terrible today.

Did I give you enough information? I can provide more if you need?

Many thanks,
Fredrick

From: cornishwitch
To: redfacedass

Hi Fred,

I didn't cast it for you yet as it seems that you may have forgotten to buy it and pay me for it? Don't worry as soon as you do this, help will be at hand.

Maria

From: redfacedass
To: cornishwitch

My dearest Maria,

I was certain I had paid you for it! I am SO sorry, I feel awful now. Well if you ever needed proof of how bad my memory really is- here you have it!!

This is what happened yesterday- I was writing the detailed description of myself (is it detailed enough for you? Perhaps I could post you a lock of hair or a toenail?), when Stephen (our dog) came scampering in from the garden with a dead mouse in his mouth. He discarded the mouse and then proceeded to shower my sofa and armchair with as much urine as he could muster. (Stephen's petulance is something else we are currently trying to deal with).

I got so angry about the bad BAD mutts behaviour that I must have forgotten to pay you the money, so please accept my humble apologies.

Why do we remember things that anger us so well, yet forget the things that please us so easily?

Not really sure how this PalPay system works yet. Can I just post you the cash?

A very sorry Fredrick

From: redfacedass
To: cornishwitch

Hi Fred,

Really, don't worry. Please don't send me a toenail urgh! LOL- I have a thing about feet haha. My address is-

Maria ****
20 ***** Street
*** ***

Let's get you sorted first, then we can deal with Stephen later. You did send me enough details.

You're of a similar age to me and so I won't ask the question as I don't want you to tell me the answer over email, but if you are a recreational drug user, you will need to avoid EVERYTHING for nine days after I cast the spell.

I will cast the spell as soon as the funds arrive and let you know what's going on...

Xx

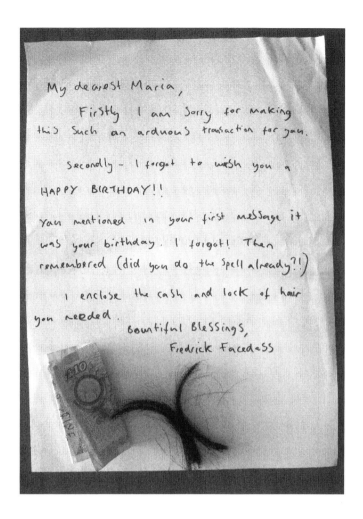

My dearest Maria,

   Firstly I am sorry for making this such an arduous transaction for you.

   Secondly - I forgot to wish you a HAPPY BIRTHDAY!!

You mentioned in your first message it was your birthday. I forgot! Then remembered (did you do the spell already?!)

   I enclose the cash and lock of hair you needed.

        Bountiful Blessings,

           Fredrick Facedass

From: redfacedass
To: cornishwitch

Dear Maria,

Hope you are having a better week than me. Tuesday went a little like this for me-

BOSS-   *"Fred do you come in. Over"*
ME-   *"Fred Here!"*
BOSS-   *"Pickup for you.... 4 Heath Road"*
ME-   *"Copy that. Over"*

1 hr later....

BOSS-   *"Where are you?"*
ME-   *"Parked up, waiting for my next fare..."*
BOSS-   *"You're supposed to be on a job now, picking up from 4 Heath Road! You're 50 minutes late!!"*
ME-   *"Sorry boss, guess it just slipped my mind..."*
BOSS-   *"YOU STUPID MAN, FRED!!!! Why don't you remember anything I say? Don't bother coming back in. You're fired."*

Yesterday I stayed in bed all day feeling sorry for myself eating Nik Naks and seedless grapes
(I hate seeded grapes). I kept thinking if only I had remembered to pay you last week then I probably wouldn't have lost my job. IF ONLY.

Maria - I sent you the letter and cash on Monday (I think) by recorded delivery so you should definitely have it by now. This morning, memory-wise, I felt a little better, but perhaps that is just psychological?

Have you had a chance to perform the spell yet? How did it go? Did you feel POWERFUL?

Please tell me it was successful. I need some hope in my life at the moment :(
Fredrick

From: cornishwitch
To: redfacedass

Hi Fred

Sorry it's taken me all day to send this. I'm dreadfully ill. :(

No, I was waiting for the payment and hair. It arrived safely this morning so I will be casting the spell tonight for you.

Sorry about your job but sometimes things happen for a reason...

So tonight when you go to sleep lay comfortably and concentrate on your breathing and make sure that now your thoughts are clear. Your mind is blank and all you hear is your own breathing and heartbeat. Now, I want you to visualise that you are walking barefoot on a sandy beach. The sand slides between your toes. You're walking slowly, it's not difficult, and it's very pleasant. As you walk along the beach, the sand between your toes, you feel the sun on your back and the gentle breeze touch the hair around your temples. You're not too hot, you are just right. You hear the waves now gently lapping at the shore and with each time that the waves come in, they bring strength and clarity to your thoughts, with each time that they go out, they take with them all of your stress, worries, negative emotions, burdens of everyday life. Nothing else exists now but you on the beach and the gentle lapping of the waves; you don't have a care in the world. When you feel empowered by the waves, I want you to say out loud-

"Venus, Goddess of all things pure, cleanse my mind as the waves cleanse this shore, make my thought now clear and sharp, and imagination and wit come with a fresh spark, help me remember all that I must, my faith's with you - in you I trust, Venus Goddess of love and light, help me in my heartfelt plight, I ask in need, I ask of thee, this is my will so may it be"

Sleep as normal now. You may have a vivid dream of a beautiful lady bringing gifts. When you awaken, you will feel refreshed, energised, calm and at peace. It's like a weight has been lifted from you and you should notice an instant change that will grow steadily over the next few days and weeks. Simply say out loud *"Venus, thank you for your gift"* even if you don't remember your dreams.

Blessings Maria

From: redfacedass
To: cornishwitch

TALIA (wife)(mine) -
"Seeing as you've got nothing to do, perhaps you could fetch some groceries for me. We need some onions, leeks, potatoes and carrots"

FREDRICK-
"No problem, back in twenty minutes"

I then returned to my happy wife clutching onto onions, leeks, potatoes, carrots, seedless grapes (I hate seeded grapes) and some Nik Naks. She embraced me.

TALIA-
"I love you my Fredrick!"

Maria- my memory is working! I cannot believe what an effect your spell has had on me; it is truly remarkable…

I said the little 'mantra' on Saturday just before I nodded myself off. I had an extremely vivid dream. Not of a beautiful goddess bringing me gifts, but I dreamt of a gang of ginger men who viciously attacked me.

No goddess. No feeling of calm and peace. Instead perhaps the worst dream I have ever had. However, it was worth it as now my memory is as astute as it could be!

I was so sorry to hear that you are unwell. You have honestly transformed my life, so I thought perhaps I could cast a spell to make you better? I have done a lot of research about this over the last few days. All I will need is a toenail clipping and the answers to the same questions you posed me and I will cast the spell for you.

I'm afraid you will have to STOP taking all the recreational drugs you like so much (please do try- it's VERY important). I am happy to do this free of charge.

Love and my brightest blessings,

Fredrick

From: cornishwitch
To: redfacedass

Oh, Fred. That is fabulous, fabulous news! And it's worked so fast for you. This will freak you out - I'm ginger!! lol

It's really great to hear of your fast results and actually, I'm all better! Maybe your wishes worked for me. I'm sitting outside a cafe bar in Italy at the moment (I'm half Italian and visiting with family here - maybe the ginger men had some bearing on me) sometimes dreams mean the opposite and that it wasn't a man attacking you but a girl helping you. It's just so strange.

I wonder if you could do me a huge favour? And I know you'll remember to do this for me now :) Could you please leave a brief testimonial in my guestbook on my 'about me' page (you can access this by clicking on my username on eBay) and just say that I cast the memory spell for you and how well and how quickly it worked - I would really appreciate this xxx

Sliding mirrored wardrobe doors x3 plus runners and tracks

Current bid **£37.00**

Enter maximum bid: Place bid

Seller info

kelly4gazzasolid (116)   Item location: Colchester
100% Positive Feedback

BEAUTIFUL looking double wardrobe with Mirrored Doors, see matching wardrobe in (see my other items) can be used together or separated to go in different bedrooms , GRAB YOURSELVES A BARGAIN!!!!!!!

Dimensions: 100cm Wide, 195cm High, 38cm Deep

Great Condistion, Grab Yourselves A Great Looking Wardrobe
Collection Only Due To Size And Weight
See My Other Items
Cash On Collection
Happy Bidding!!!!!!

From: redfacedass
To: kelly4gazzasolid

Dear kelly4gazzasolid,

How are you getting on? I'm great (thanks).

What lovely robe mirrors you have. We have ones just like it.

Today I have being reminiscing over items of furniture from my past. (I've just seen a bedside table that I grew up with from the age of 7!)

I have recently lost my job and hence have a LOT of time on my hands and really not much to do with it.

I couldn't help noticing, in the reflection of your lovely mirrors, that your bedroom looks a bit of a state and in desperate need of some TLC... I assume that you are rather busy with your job (and life) and so have been forced to neglect the room (I understand). Seeing as I am not busy at all, I thought I could offer my services...

I could pop round and redecorate it for you. I wouldn't expect any money for this. I am just genuinely quite bored and REALLY like to help people out.

Friendly Regards,

Fredrick Facedass

P.S I have 2.6 litres of spare magnolia

From: kelly4gazzasolid
To: redfacedass

Dear Fred Sadass,

This photo was actually taken before our decorating was done. ITS DONE NOW, we have also got new wardrobes TO COMPLIMENT THE NEW DECOR, we have transformed it into a beautiful BOUDOIR, AS I LOVE ART AND DESIGN AND CAN DECORATE, but hey thanks for the offer, but the job in hand is finally complete, oh magnolia is sooo boring and not me, its too council house looking, i like rich and warm colours, and my taste is designer and chic decor, im sure there are people out there you could help who like magnolia, i do hope you find work, so you can be happy and not so bored.

kind regards

kellycandecorate.co.uk

From: redfacedass
To: kelly4gazzasolid

Dear kellycandecorate.co.uk,

Thanks for your hasty reply! Sorry I was unable to get back to you sooner, I have been kept quite busy the last few days helping a neighbour (Beatrice) de-leaf her gutters (quite problematic at this time of year).

My name is Fredrick Facedass- not Fred Sadass. At first, I thought that you were trying to insult me, but then I noticed how awful the grammar was throughout your message, and so I assume it was just a mistake (?)

It's ok- I too didn't know anything about English language and grammar when I first moved here from Cyprus… Whereabouts are you from? How long have you been in England?

Growing up in a council flat, my mother always painted the walls with magnolia!!! How did you know that? (I guess design has never really been a strong point for the Facedass family!!).

I have spoken with Talia (my wife) about our little chat and she has got it into her head that I MUST redecorate the living room. Guess what… she wants the *Designer/Chic* look too!

I'll be honest- I don't really know what the *Designer/Chic* look is? I thought perhaps you could help me with any advice (colour schemes etc), or you could even just send me a picture of your place and I'll just copy from that.

In return for your expert design advice-I could help you get settled into English grammar?

Talia and I are REALLY excited to hear about your decoration tips and a photo of your beautiful boudoir!

I tried putting kellycandecorate.co.uk into Google, but there doesn't appear to be a website? Guess that's a work in progress for you? Gosh, you are a busy girl!

Look forward to hearing from you soon,
Fred

From: redfacedass

To: kelly4gazzasolid

Dear kellycandecorate.co.uk,

How's it all going?
I've been rather busy again!

I did have time to pick out some colours for the living room just wondered what you thought of them? I'm thinking perhaps 'Dulux Lemon Pie' for the walls and the 'Dulux Windsor Blue' for the skirting and woodwork etc.

I am REALLY keen to get you up to speed with English grammar- perhaps we could have a session of emailed correspondence? Starting with a little lesson in the 'Three *Theres*' (there, their and they're). You should find it useful.

When are you free over the next few days? My movements are as follows-

MONDAY (today)-
A.M   Analysing products on eBay
P.M   Making dinner (toad in the hole)

TUESDAY-
A.M   FREE TIME
P.M   Helping neighbour with enlargement of cat flap (to accommodate a small dog)

Nb. It MIGHT be possible for me to move my allotted eBay time in to a free time slot if it helps with your schedule.

Regards Fred

From: kelly4gazzasolid

To: redfacedass

Leave me alone.

"I'm Not Racist, But I Hate Gingers" Funny T-Shirt

Quantity: **24 available**

Price: **£9.99**

Seller info

bigdogtshirts (353)   Item location: Watford

99.7% Positive Feedback

"I'M NOT RACIST! BUT I HATE GINGERS"

Make sure you choose the right size from our shop
Chest sizes are shown -

sml - 36" med - 38" lge - 40" x: 42" - 44"

From: redfacedass
To: bigdogtshirts

Dear Bigdogtshirts,

I have a new hobby- analysing products on eBay. This morning I came across this T-Shirt and I really feel that the item is not in good spirit.

Hating Gingers is a form of racism, just the same as hating someone for the colour of their skin.

Yours faithfully,

Mr Facedass

From: bigdogtshirts
To: redfacedass

Hi,

Thank you for your comments on this item. I am also ginger and have explained this to several people. The idea came from comments that I received from friends and other people.
Regards
Simon

From: redfacedass
To: bigdogtshirts

Dear Simon,

Don't call me ginger. I HATE GINGERS.

Regards,
Fredrick Facedass

What's that all about then??? Do you want a T- Shirt???

Dear Simon,

Could I have a medium sized t-shirt with the sentence-*'I hate a ginger man called Simon'* printed across the chest area?

Can I please have all the letters in lower case, except for the first letter of your name (S) (Simon)?
I shall leave the choice of font up to you. I trust your good judgement.
Please post to-

Fredrick Facedass
**** **** St
** ***

Regards,
Mr Facedass

From: bigdogtshirts
To: redfacedass

Yes- I can do that. Pay £12.50 to- simon@********.co.uk and I'll get it out to you.

From: redfacedass
To: bigdogtshirts

Simon!

Here is a picture of me in my new t-shirt. I love it. It's all I ever wear.

I'm looking for new work, so perhaps you might like to use this photo for advertising and promotional purposes? I imagine this new design will prove popular. I would only require a small fee for modelling your T-Shirts (£12).

Many Thanks,

Freddy

P.S- you were so right to overrule my request for the lower casing, as I think it looks fantastic in capitals. Congrats for that.

Italian Charms- "Oh My God!!"

Quantity: **9 available**

Price: **£1.25**   Buy it now

Seller info
tigercharms (1224 ⚫)   Item location: Oxford
100% Positive Feedback

9mm Laser Charm

This charm is compatible with all brands of 9mm Italian Bracelet

these links are spring loaded and can stretch to fit your wrist
Visit My eBay Shop for more great charms, Necklaces,
Watches, Key rings, Bracelets and mobile phone dangles

From: redfacedass
To: tigercharms

Dear Tigercharms,

This is the second product on eBay that I have found (VERY) offensive today. What sort of lessons are you teaching to children? You should really respect other people's beliefs even if you don't share the same view as them.

Do you think that it's nice selling blasphemous goods? Some people may well be offended.

Regards Fredrick

From: tigercharms
To: redfacedass

We also have the charms 'as if...' and 'Whatever' available.

We do custom made charms too, but I think 'Small Minded Religious Zealot' may be a bit of a squeeze.

VEGGIE / VEGAN WRISTBAND- PROMOTE THE CAUSE

Quantity: **20 available**

Price: **£2.22**   Buy it now

Seller info

veg-bands (146)   Item location: London

100% Positive Feedback

A visible wristband promoting a cause close to your heart

What better way to show your true colours?

These are the original wristbands, which will publically demonstrate YOUR solidarity and support for the vegetarian/ vegan way of life.

Each band comes individually packaged and will be mailed within 24 hours.

From: redfacedass
To: veg-bands

Dear Veg-bands,

If we aren't supposed to eat animals, why on earth are they made from meat?

Fredrick Facedass

From: veg-bands
To: redfacedass

DEAR RED FACED ASS

I am sure you don't expect me to justify your antagonistic question with an answer, but I will anyway. Animals are made of FLESH and other things. If you choose to eat them, well that is your choice. Me, I choose a more compassionate lifestyle, which is also the most healthy. But, each to their own…

From: redfacedass
To: veg-bands

Dear Veg-bands,

My name is Fredrick (Fred for short or Red for VERY short) Facedass (my surname of Greek Cypriot origin) (pronounced Fass-e-dass). Not the offensive name that you greeted me with in your recent message.

Vegetarianism is something that is so peculiar to me, almost unfathomable. I was brought up on a very VERY healthy diet- nearly every meal consisted of meat. Hams with cheese and bread for breakfast, for lunch perhaps some fish, and for dinner often a 'stifado' a traditional Cypriot stew made from beef or dog with red wine and tomatoes. My question to you was genuine, and I am hurt that you found it to be antagonistic.

I must say, I found your response to be a touch self-righteous- 'a more compassionate lifestyle' etc. I urge you to give meat a chance before your condition gets any worse, like Vegonism for example.

Regards

Red (Fred) Facedass

From: veg-bands
To: redfacedass

Dear Frederick.

I apologise if I misunderstood your username and put the spaces in the wrong place.

Αυτά μου φαίνονται κινέζικα.

I too was brought up eating a typical Western diet of meat and two veg. It was what my mother was lead to believe was the healthiest thing for us, and what at the time, we didn't know better about. I have since done some extensive research, and have discovered that actually, meat is not good for us, certainly not in the quantities that most people in the West consume it.

I definitely feel better now that I don't eat meat, and I am the healthiest person compared to all my counterparts who do eat meat. With regards to who comes down with colds and flu and bugs etc - I've not had a day off work.

I also believe that I am doing the compassionate thing and not contributing to animal suffering. I've been vegan for seven years, so I don't contribute to the cruelty that is the dairy industry either. If you would like more information, perhaps you could order yourself the DVD called Earthlings, and also one called Truth Or Dairy. I am sure you'll find them to be eye opening.

Give peas a chance-

Kind vegan regards Abi

From: redfacedass
To: veg-bands

Dearest Abi,

I understand that maybe this was a simple misjudgement on your behalf- it was all a bit foreign to you. I must admit though I found you writing 'it's all Greek to me' in Greek rather confusing…

I couldn't determine if you meant this as some sort of ironic joke. Or, if you do speak Greek, you were demonstrating to me that it wasn't 'All Greek' to you at all, and therefore calling me a 'Red Faced Ass' was actually completely intentional.

My line of thinking at present is that you were making an ironic joke. If this is the case, I will take joy in the form of laughter as that is a most witty thing you did. If, however, I am mistaken and it was the latter of the two, then please disregard everything I am now about to say, for our relationship is DEAD.

I have therefore decided to forgive your rudeness. I see now that it was merely a mistake.

I took your advice and watched the DVD called Truth Or Dairy. Whilst I found this to be a mite dated, and hated the house/dance music, it was very informative. As you put it a real eye opener!

With regards to the health issue- I spoke with a vegon former colleague of mine, whom I had never really spoken much with ((for meat eating reasons) and hygiene reasons too). He also seemed to share the same feelings as you- he is never ill and always feels full of beans.

My wife thinks that I'm crazy, but I have decided that I will be attempting a sponsored 'Vegon Week'.

During VEGON WEEK I will eat and drink only what your kind consider 'right'. The aim of this week is both to raise awareness for vegonism and, through donations, some money to be given to a suitable vegon charity (perhaps you could recommend one?) I have purchased one of your vegon wristbands and will wear it for the duration of my sponsored week.

I look forward to hearing what you think of the new me!

Your friend Freddy

From: veg-bands
To: redfacedass

Dearest Fred,

I do apologise again for calling you Red Faced Ass - I genuinely thought that was your username.

I don't actually speak Greek, I'm afraid. I looked up how to say 'it's all Greek to me'. I am really glad it brought a smile to your face and my wit was not wasted.

I'm genuinely flattered that you went and watched Truth or Dairy. I went vegan without watching it, and haven't actually even seen it, though I understand it is quite enlightening, so that is why I felt able to suggest it, even though I'd not seen it myself. I had also heard it was a bit out-dated, but if the info is still relevant, I suppose that is good.

I'm also very chuffed you feel moved enough to try out this vegan lark if only for a week.
That's brilliant. :-)
I wish you very well with your little project, and hope you feel great on it. Are you going completely cold-turkey? Ironic expression, huh! :-)

The Vegan Society is a charity - I suppose that would be the ideal one?
Or something like the NSPCC - they aren't vegan, but it's nice to help children.

Does your vegan colleague have bad personal hygiene?????
And how did you stumble upon veggie wristbands on eBay anyway??? I am just intrigued! Have a lovely day, and if I can help with your week with guidance and support, let me know.

Kind vegan regards

Abi

From: redfacedass
To: veg-bands

My Abi, (is that short for Abigail or Abisola or perhaps something else??)

Abi, I must say you are quite the joker- you seem to have wit in abundance. I found the 'cold turkey' joke in particular extremely funny, and feel like I am starting to get to know you. I would also like to apologise for getting so furious about the whole 'Red Faced Ass' issue we once had. I can now assure you that issue is done with and in actual fact I think I quite like you :)

I came across veg-bands purely by chance. I was trying to find a copy of Suzanne Vega's- Solitude Standing on CD. I have always thought she was called Suzanne Vegon! And so my search led me to all these vegon and vegetarian products. This infuriated the once naive me, as Vegons and Vegetarians were people I once considered foe.

Sebastian does indeed have personal hygiene problems. I was under the impression that the body odour was perhaps a by-product of his dreadful diet? He has assured me this is nothing to do with his diet, and actually seemed quite offended that I'd asked him! I'm left only to assume he has elected to wear dirty ill-fitting clothes and to not clean himself adequately.

Thank you for all your good wishes and I will be sure to keep you up to date with my progress.

Say Kerpow to cow- your friend Freddy

From: veg-bands
To: redfacedass

You are hilarious and I don't know quite what to make of you! It's kinda weird being so emaily with someone I don't really know! Or do I!?

Abisola? I like that. But no, it's Abigail.

Ah, Freddy the Red- you flatter me with kind comments about my wit! But thank you! Blush! I'm glad you found the cold turkey comment amusing- I do try! I was going to go the whole hog and ask if you were going to go the whole hog all at once, but I thought one joke at a time was enough. :-)

Suzanne Vega should be vegan, if she is not already. I would have gone vegan ages ago if I had a name like that!

I am sorry that Sebastian smells and has potentially given vegans a bad rep. I can assure you that I smell sweet as flowers and fruit and chocolate, depending on what I showered with in the morning. Hmm, I guess some vegans do go all hippy and think it's cool to have matted hair and not use soap, but not this one. I look and smell very normal. I think!

Kerpow to cow is now going to be incorporated into several of my emails from now on. Kerpow- see!

Btw, there is a vegan Fayre happening THIS WEEKEND (well, Sunday) in Kensington- if you are at a loose end, maybe you could check it out. You will find lots of lovely vegan chocolate and cheese and pretend meats (e.g. vegan fake bacon)

All the best, my new little friend

Abi

From: redfacedass
To: veg-bands

VEGON WEEK-   DAY ONE

7.20- Breakfast

2 pieces of toast
2 fake bacon (from Kensington fayre)
1 cup of tea (black)

11.00- Elevenses

1 soya latte
1 special fruity vegon biscuit (from Kensington fayre)

13.30- Lunch

1 lettuce and tomato sandwich (on rye bread)
1 golden delicious apple
1 bottle of sparkling water

19.04- Dinner (late)

8 Linda McCartney (brand) Sausages
4 crushed potatoes
1 slice pretend chocolate cake (from fayre)

23.50- bedtime tea (camomile)

From: veg-bands
To: redfacedass

Hi Fred,

That's great! How are you finding it?

I was at Kensington Fayre too. What did you make of it all?
Hope you had a nice day. I won't be able to email much for a
while as I am out of the office on jury service for goodness
knows how long!

Hope you like your new wristband!

Cheers Abi

P.S What was your chocolate cake pretending to be?

From: redfacedass
To: veg-bands

VEGON WEEK-   DAY TWO

5.45 - Breakfast (early)

8 bowls 'Jordan's- the super foods breakfast flakes' (with
soya milk)
1 cup of tea (white)(soya milk)
1 glass orange juice (with bits)
4 bananas

<u>9.30- Elevenses (v early)</u>

1 soya latte
4 special fruity vegon biscuit (from fayre)
13 apples (9 golden delicious, 4 pink ladies)

<u>13.30- Lunch</u>

17 pieces of falafel in pitta with salad and spicy sauce
65 seedless grapes (I hate seeded grapes)
1 banana
1 bottle of sparkling water

<u>19.09- Dinner (late)</u>

19 Linda McCartney (brand) Deep Country Pies
40 chips
1 glass pressed apple juice
2 slices pretend chocolate cake ((from fayre) pretending to contain egg, milk and other crucial ingredients)

00.11- bedtime tea (camomile)

From: redfacedass
To: veg-bands

<u>VEGON WEEK-   DAY THREE</u>

Abi I'm sorry.

I really did try, but I was just WAY too hungry...........

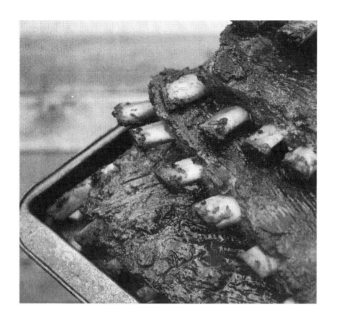

EARN £1000 A DAY. 100% GUARANTEED WORK, WITH FULL SUPPORT

Quantity: **200 available**

Price: **£5.95**   [Buy it now]

Seller info
davemacca (146)   Item location: London
100% Positive Feedback

Hi my name is Dave Macca,
I'm 28 years old... And I work 2 - 3 hours a week

I can show you how to make £31,000 - £60,000 per month...
I hope you're ready for this - all you need to click and buy
I'm going to show you how you can copy
my £1,000 per day system

It took me from the verge of bankruptcy to being
financially secure in just a YEAR AND A HALF

From: redfacedass
To: davemacca

Hello Dave,

My wife says enough is enough- I need to get a job, so I'm contacting you regarding the fantastic opportunity advertised on eBay.

I am VERY attracted by the £1000 per day. To be honest I've only ever earned a little more than that per month, so such a high wage is very appealing to me.

I've attached my CV for your consideration.

Please don't leap to the conclusion from my CV that I'm a 'job hopper'. Yes, I have had over 20 jobs in my time, but I have never ever quit a job.

I'm happy to come and meet with you to discuss further. Very much look forward to hearing from you at your earliest convenience.

Kindest regards,

Fredrick Frascuelo Facedass

Fredrick Frascuelo Facedass
Curriculum vitae

19th May 1973

WORK:
February to present; unemployed
Previous job; Taxi Driver

Pre-previous job; 19 different jobs across various fields. It would be too boring to list all of these.

QUALIFICATIONS:
Provisional Driving Licence

REASON FOR LEAVING PREVIOUS EMPLOYERS:
Constant forgetfulness led to my dismissal. A witch on eBay has since fixed my memory, so this is no longer a problem for us. Seriously, don't worry.

PERSONAL INTERESTS:
Donating blood. Twenty-five pints thus far.
Charity work- I've recently done some fundraising for Vegons.
Helping people with handy-work and being a good person.

From: davemacca
To: redfacedass

Hello Fredrick,

Thanks for your email, I am not advertising a `job' what I offer is an established home business which is suitable for anyone looking for extra income.

Should you be interested you can order your copy from the listing.

Regards,

Dave Macca

From: redfacedass
To: davemacca

Dear Dave,

Thanks for taking the time to read my application.

I'm encouraged to hear that you'd take me on, I was a little worried that my CV lacked computer based experience, but I guess I'm using a computer to write to you now, aren't I?

I'm really delighted to accept the position at your 'established home business'. I promise not to refer to it as a 'job' again (guess this is a tax avoidance thing). Mum's the word ;)

I've already told my wife about my new 'job' (sorry) and she is over the moon. She really can't believe that I'll be earning SO much. I've just worked out that you earn £2300 per hour! I really don't know why everyone doesn't do this job- it's amazing!

The commute to your home in Oxford isn't too bad either- looks like it will take me just over an hour to get to you.

I promise that I'll be a really hard worker. Is there a uniform I should wear?

Kindest regards

Fred

From: davemacca
To: redfacedass

Dear Fred,

You seem to have the wrong idea here, please let me explain. This is NOT a job!

I offer home-based business ideas to individuals to run from their own homes NOT from mine.

Please do not visit my private address this is not what this about. Should you wish to buy the business I am offering then please order from the listing.

Regards

Dave Macca

From: redfacedass
To: davemacca

Dear Dave,

Is working at your place definitely out of the question? My wife is VERY keen for me to get a job anywhere that's not our house! (Think I'm getting under her feet a little…)

If that's really not an option, my wife may consider letting me set up office in our basement, but thought I'd better check with you first?

I've attached a plan of my proposed office space- let me know what you think.

Can't wait to get started for you boss. Let's bring home the bacon!

Best regards,
Fred

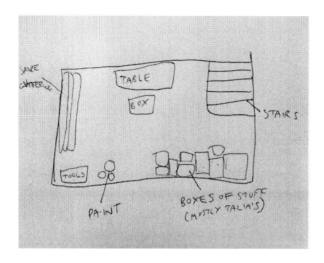

From: davemacca
To: redfacedass

There is NO job here for you.

DO NOT buy this product. It is NOT suitable for you.

LEATHER MASK, BONDAGE, DOG HIGH QUALITY LOCKABLE

Quantity: **20 available**

Price: **£20.98**   Buy it now

Seller info
dominantwear (120)   Item location: Yorkshire
100% Positive Feedback

Heavy Duty leather Hood You are bidding on a high quality leather hood/mask with dog features, this mask is perfect for puppy play or just fun in the bedroom. This mask is made from faux leather but is very strong and very durable.

One size fits 95% as the hood is fully adjustable at the back.

From: redfacedass
To: dominantwear

Dear Dominantwear,

I was wondering if you might be able to help me.

Could you tell me for what reason one might wear this mask?

I only ask as the other day I was leaving my house to collect some guttering brackets from B&Q (my neighbour's guttering became loose after it was badly de-leafed), and when I pulled off up the road I noticed in the rear-view mirror, my wife going into our house with a gentleman and a two-toned dog with hands like a man.

At the time I didn't think too much of it and when I got back, with the gutter brackets, my wife immediately put my mind at rest, saying it had been Roger and Sparky (his Alsatian) from up the road popping round to see if we will sign a petition against yet another new Tesco opening.

I trust my wife, but now thinking about it- dogs don't have hands do they? More importantly Sparky doesn't have hands either (although he is two-toned).

I've been searching all over the internet for a dog with a leathery face like the one on my drive two days ago and then I came across you. The dogface you are selling matches exactly the same dogface I saw…

Regards
Fredrick Facedass

From: dominantwear
To: redfacedass

Cheers Fred for the message and pardon my ignorance towards not seeing the relevance of your point

From: redfacedass
To: dominantwear

Dear Dominantwear,

I wouldn't call you ignorant, perhaps unaware, but not ignorant...

There have been some developments on the two-toned, leathery dogface front...

This morning I spied the mongrel again driving down our street. Having already spotted this weird dog on my drive the other week, I put two and two together and figured that he had come from my home. Now I've seen him driving I know for certain that this is actually a human wearing a leather dog mask (like the one you are selling) and not a dog with hands after all!

When I got home my wife was nursing a sore bottom (she'd sat down badly). Contrary to my suspicions- she said that there hadn't been a man with a leathery dogface at our home.

We've had a few ups and downs recently, but I do trust her. However, when you see a man with a leathery dogface twice in such quick succession the mind does start to wonder...

Would you be suspicious of my wife if you were in my situation? I would really appreciate your advice.

Kindest regards
Fred

From: dominantwear
To: redfacedass

Fred, are you for real lol, I will say one thing, you tell a hell of a good story, why don't you buy a mask put it on, knock on the door when your wife is in alone, when she lets you in, just see what happens, then your mind will be put to rest, result!!

From: redfacedass
To: dominantwear

Dear Dominantwear,

I feel a bit rude, as I haven't asked how you are. How are you?

I still don't know your name either! Yes I am for real- I'm writing to you right this very instant. I can assure you this isn't a story and this is very much happening to me.

I haven't seen our leathery dog-faced friend since we last spoke, but I'm convinced he will return…

I've been thinking long and hard about what you said and I'm starting to think what a good idea it would be to don the dogface mask myself. Well done!

I've recently lost my job and as you can imagine things are a little hard for me. I will only need the mask for a day to try and find out what dogface's game is. So, would you consider renting this mask out to me?

I have plenty of free time since losing my job and I often find myself at a loose end, so if you need any assistance with anything, feel free to ask.

Kind regards Fredrick

From: dominantwear
To: redfacedass

Fred,

I trust you will not mind me calling you Fred? How much would you like to loan one for? Just so I can have a look at the costs etc...

Regards, Patrick

From: redfacedass
To: dominantwear

Patrick,

Thanks for putting your trust in me- you were right to do so, as I love people calling me Fred! I was thinking perhaps £3.00 per day (same as my local video shop) would be fair. I would cover your postage too.

Many thanks for your suggestion and future loan. Fred

From: dominantwear
To: redfacedass

Hi Fred,

Apologies for the delay, I have just returned home from being down country on business, in relation to your offer, I cannot offer a rental scheme for you but what I can suggest is that you purchase the item from the shop, I will credit your account with £7.00, how's that for an offer?

As you will respect I cannot offer rentals as once the item has been worn I cannot accept returns, which I'm sure you will appreciate.

Just stick to the plan I put to you and you will not go far wrong.

Best regards,
Patrick

From: redfacedass
To: dominantwear

Patrick,

I've done some maths and I've worked out that a 1-day rental (at £3) would actually end up costing me £11 after the delivery and return!! Your offer of a £7 refund brings the price down to £13.98. Whilst I really can't afford to spend

£13.98 at the moment- it's actually only £2.98 more expensive than the rental program I had proposed…

So, I can't really argue with your (moderately) kind offer.

I have made the payment through your site and put my trust in you to return £7 to my PayPal account. If you could please post it ASAP I would very much appreciate it.

Thank you for the plan and your assistance in these difficult times.

Kind regards,
Your friend Fredrick

From: dominantwear
To: redfacedass

Hi Fred,

Thanks for getting in touch, I will send your item out on Monday and once positive feedback has been left towards us I will be more than happy to credit you the 7 pound as promised and agreed,

Best regards,
Patrick

From: redfacedass
To: dominantwear

Patrick,

Hope you are well. The mask arrived successfully on Saturday (thanks!)

THE PLAN-

On Friday I am entering the World Pooh Sticks tournament, so I am going to be away for the day. But, (and this is the crucial part) I told Talia that the contest is on THURSDAY! She thinks I'll be away on Thursday.

So, Thursday morning I will head off on my supposed 'World Pooh Sticks' trip, only to return wearing the dog-faced mask and surprise Talia. Good plan, don't you think?

I did try the mask on in secret (away from Talia) down in the basement. And, I am really struggling to see why people wear these?!

How on earth does one relax in a leathery dog-faced mask? It's so claustrophobic?

Regards Fred

From: dominantwear
To: redfacedass

Fred,

Hope you are well too? In relation to advice on how to wear the item unfortunately I am unable to advise, stick to plan that was mentioned and you will not go far wrong.

Best regards,

Patrick

From: redfacedass
To: dominantwear

Patrick,

How's it going? Sorry not to be in touch- been really busy helping out some neighbours with their rogue hedges.

Firstly- I should announce that I am now the current World Pooh Stick champion! But, it's the day before my victory that I need to tell you about...

Arriving back at the house wearing the leathery dog-faced mask, I was extremely nervous and unsure about what I might find. What I saw was Talia in a white mask and the leathery dog-faced man in our garden not wearing very much at all…

Initially I was VERY shocked at this sight, but Talia said she could explain everything (I have to admit that at this point, I was starting think that something might possibly be up). But, Talia told me that she and Mike (leathery-faced-dog-man) were rehearsing for a play (the name of which she had forgotten) to be performed in our local church hall, and the reason they were naked (except masks) was that they were both far too hot (it was a lovely sunny day (I hope you enjoyed the sunshine?)). She hadn't wanted to tell me about the play previously- in case I disapproved.

Silly me for doubting her! I should have known all along there would be a simple explanation…

Mike seemed like a really lovely man with a big strong chest. I even managed to get a quick group photo of us together. I wanted to take a few more pictures to be safe, but Mike seemed to be in a bit of rush to head off and Talia didn't want to sit down too long for more pictures (sore bottom).

Anyway just thought I should keep you up to date and let you know how well your plan worked.

Many thanks,
Your pal Fredrick

Mike (Left), Talia (centre), Fredrick (me) (right)

From: dominantwear
To: redfacedass

Fred,

I trust you are well?

Many thanks for getting back to me. It is much appreciated.

I'm sure it's all above board, but Mike's eyes do look a little suspicious though. I can't really tell with Talia as her face is too covered, you must have more shots of the event though?

Speak soon,
Patrick

Portrait of Kevin Costner

Current bid   **£0.00**

Enter maximum bid:

Place bid

Seller info

newdali (221)   Item location: Brighton

100% Positive Feedback

KEVIN COSTNER (DRAWING)
14CM X 14CM

Comes as displayed
Fast delivery
Thank you very much

From: redfacedass
To: newdali

Dear New Dali,

Hope you are keeping well.

I've been looking through your artwork and I have to say I'm really impressed (great stuff). I was totally blown away by your drawing of Kevin Costner; you've captured him perfectly. Well done.

I seem to have upset my wife by (wrongfully) suggesting that she was having an affair with a leathery dog-faced man. Now I really need to show her how much I love and trust her...

It's our 10-year anniversary very soon and I think if I can do something really special for her.

If I were to commission a very talented artist (you) to draw a portrait of us- I think that could be just the present for her.

What do you say- will you draw us? (I can get a photograph over to you.)

Btw, where did you train?

Look forward to hearing from you,

Fredrick Facedass

From: newdali

To: redfacedass

Send me Several Photos of you together (Roughly Five) and I will see what I can do. I'm terrified of Pressure but as long as it's possible, I'll see if I can capture you. If I can't, you'll understand. Train, Train my dear boy, I didn't train, I acquired my gifts naturally.

From: redfacedass
To: newdali

Dear New Dali,

Hope you are keeping well.

Sorry not to get back to you right away- I've been busy looking after a distraught neighbour; they've just been the victims of a nasty burglary. The cheeky crooks managed to get in through the cat flap (which has been enlarged to accommodate their dog) and stole pretty much everything. Can you believe the insurance isn't going to pay a penny either (because of the dog flap)!

I'm so pleased that you are willing to do this artwork. Talia will be so happy. Please don't put any pressure on yourself though, but this could just about save our marriage…

I've emailed a few pictures for you. I quite like the one of us taken at Christmas - mainly because I was less fat then, but you're the artist and should have the final say.

If you could produce something even half as good as your Kevin Costner picture- I'd be over the moon!

Look forward to hearing from you.

Kind regards
Fredrick

From: newdali
To: redfacedass

Here you are. Follow the link and buy-

Portrait

Current bid **£5.50**

Enter maximum bid:

Place bid

Seller info

newdall (221)
100% Positive Feedback

Item location: Brighton

Bespoke portrait

From: redfacedass
To: newdali

Great- that looks fantastic! Talia will be so happy. I'm putting the payment through to you right this second. Thanks.

From: newdali
To: redfacedass

1st class tomorrow :)

From: redfacedass
To: newdali

Hello,

How you doing? I'm not doing too well to be honest (THIS IS NOT YOUR FAULT THOUGH).

Firstly- thanks for getting the picture across to me. I framed it and gave it a prominent position on the shelves next to the phone and takeaway menus. I left it there ready as a surprise for her to find. THIS WAS A MISTAKE!

It turns out the lady in the picture wasn't Talia. I had been so concerned with how I looked in the photo that I forgot to check who the other person was! I actually gave you a picture of me with my ex girlfriend (think you'll agree that my ex was quite a sort?) taken many years ago.

It's really sad because I wanted the day to be perfect. I wanted to show her how much I love and trust her.

Do stay in touch.

Fredrick

CONKERS- ten in number freshly picked

Starting bid **£0.99**

Enter maximum bid: [_____] Place bid

Seller info
crabbiejoe (918)   Item location: Pontefract
100% Positive Feedback

YOU ARE BIDDING ON TEN
FRESHLY PICKED CONKERS.

THEY ARE OF A GOOD SIZE FOR CONKERING OR
PLANTING, I HAVE MORE IF REQUIRED

THANKS FOR LOOKING

PLEASE LOOK AT MY OTHER ITEMS

From: redfacedass
To: crabbyjoe

Dear Crabby Joe,

I have spent several days now searching for conkers. I HAVE FOUND NONE. This weekend I am entered into the WCC (World Conker Championships) in Northamptonshire.

Does your wife ever use the phrases- 'it's something to do' or 'it will do you good to get out of the house'? It seems those are the only phrases my wife ever uses!

This weekend I am making a 200 mile round-trip, to make battle with a conker. (My wife signs me up quite regularly on all kinds of long distance trips at the weekends. Secretly I think she likes a bit of peace and quiet!)

Crabby Joe at this stage I would like to point out that I am currently the WPS (World Pooh Sticks) Champion. I was a novice at the sport until only a month ago, you see Crabby Joe I am FIERCELY competitive.

Many (one) people (person) told me that luck won me my previous contest. NOT true.

Studying the flow of the river on the days leading up to the WPS contest, I was able to work out exactly the right place to land my stick. On the big day I arrived 9 hours early for the contest to take my pre-planned position. I wore 15 layers of clothes and stuffed sheets, towels and other laundry up my top to increase my body mass. This kept others competitors away from the 'prime' spot and me. (It was pretty darn hot though!)

Crabby Joe, I am telling you this so you can understand HOW important this is to me. I will stop at nothing to win this competition.

Are your conkers good enough for me (a World Champion) to wield?

Do you have any advice on hardening conkers or special techniques? Any advice would be massively appreciated.

Regards Fredrick

From: crabbyjoe
To: redfacedass

AY UP FRED HOWS THA GOING ME OLD MUKKER, HAS YOUR LASS ENTERNED THA IN THE WELLY THROWING UP ERE IN YORKSHIRE AS WELL, SHE COULD EVEN GET YA FARTHER AWAY IN DEEPEST YORKSHIRE, I AV GOT THREE HUNDRED WELLIES FOR SALE AS WELL IF THA WANTS, THE ALL LEFT FOOTED THO, AY THE MIGHT JUST SUIT THEE. LET US KNOW. OH BY THE WAY GOT LOADS OF CONKERS AS WELL, JUST RATE FOR THEE MATCH.

TO HARDEN SOAK IN VINEGAR BUT BEWARE U MAY GET DONE IF SPOTTED BY THE RIGHT PERSON, HAVE YOUR LOOKOUTS STRATEGICALLY PLACED.

CRABBYJOE (ONE WORD PLEASE)

MAY I BID YOU A VERY GOODNIGHT AND KIND REGARDS.

From: redfacedass
To: crabbyjoe

Dear Crabbyjoe (1 word)(sorry),

I had been looking at a number of sellers and have now decided that yours are the ones for me.

Crabbyjoe, what I would like you to do for me is to pick out the BEST 5 you can find.

If you give me your PayPal details I will get a fiver off to you.

I have not been entered into the WWW (World Wellie Wanging) Championships yet, but I'm sure the wife will have me doing that next year!! I believe the big contest is in Finland, so that's surely a week's trip away :(

Thanks for the vinegar tip off! I have since researched this further, and found that the vinegar has a tightening effect upon the molecules- shrinking the conker and making it denser.

Is there a particular type of vinegar that you would recommend?

Hope you are having a pleasant day.
Fredrick

From: crabbyjoe
To: redfacedass

Dear redfacedass,

Now then Fred me old son, *********@talk.com and will post today if before 5, cheers, let me know address

From: redfacedass
To: crabbyjoe

Crabbyjoe,

Money should be with you now old-boy! Please post to-
Fredrick Facedass
**** St
** ***

Off out to get some vinegar now! What do you reckon-Malt vinegar or maybe even a wine or cider vinegar??

Thanks for your help,

Fredrick Facedass

From: redfacedass
To: crabbyjoe

Dear Crabbyjoe,

What a weekend!

I am currently writing to you from the laptop as I am now living down in the basement. My wife (Talia) is up in the main house with Stephen (our dog).

I am staying down here until I get my head clear.

On Saturday I returned home the World Conker Champion. I also returned home earlier than Talia expected to a party that was lets just say in 'full swing'.

It seems Talia has been enjoying swinger's parties, whilst I have been away, with leathery-dog-faced people on a regular basis. May 12th (day I was crowned World Pooh Sticks Champion) was another date she held a party. I'm sure there have been many more too.

It has become apparent that the trips Talia has been sending me on were entirely for her own enjoyment. Not mine.

I would like to thank you for choosing me such a superb conker. I soaked the little beauty in vinegar overnight before baking it in the oven and we smashed our way through all competition.

Unfortunately, this victory has been slightly marred by the discovery of my wife having group sex with many men dressed in faux leather dog masks.

I am just spending my time down here on the computer whilst I decide what's for the best. It's a really difficult decision because I really do love her.

Thanks again for all your help.

Best regards,
Fredrick

From: crabbyjoe
To: redfacedass

Fred

I am really glad you got the conkers and u won including my little vinegar tip. So your wife is a swinger then. Don't you want to indulge with her?

Do please keep in touch- crabbyjoe

Electrolux Vacuum Cleaner - for parts or spares - collection only

Current bid **£0.99**

Enter maximum bid:

Place bid

Seller info

gazthemaz (77)
100% Positive Feedback

Item location: Macclesfield

Vacuum cleaner no longer working.

Selling for spares/repairs/parts.

COLLECTION ONLY - MACCLESFIELD

From: redfacedass
To: gazthemaz

Hello Gazthemaz,

Hope you are well.

I caught my wife cheating on me last weekend, so I've decided to get out of London and head up to Macclesfield for the weekend.

I'm going to visit an old aunty that I haven't seen for some time on Saturday and I thought perhaps I could come round and fix your Vacuum with you on Sunday. You could then re-list it as working and sell it for more:)

Since I lost my job I've been helping out neighbours with odd jobs. Helping you out with this would help take my mind off things at home, so really you'd be doing me a favour!

Look forward to meeting you,
Fredrick

From: gazthemaz
To: redfacedass

Hello Fredrick,

Thanks for your message. Sorry I didn't reply sooner. I've been very busy at work and only just saw it now.

I really appreciate your offer, but someone has already put a bid on it so I will sell it as it is now.

Also, I have some friends coming over to stay this weekend and we have something planned to do on Sunday.

I hope you have a good trip to see your Aunty; maybe you can do something with her on Sunday if you haven't seen her for a long time?

Like I say, thanks again but I will simply sell it as not working.

Regards Gareth

Iphone 6 (used)

Enlarge

Current bid **£35.00**

Enter maximum bid: [   ] Place bid

Seller info

pete j (98 ★)

100% Positive Feedback

Item location: Macclesfield

Item description

You are bidding on a iphone 6 mobile Phone which is used.
The phone is in good condition apart from a few scratches.
It is 7 months old and I'm selling as I no longer need it.

Includes
+iphone 6
+box
+instructions
+mains charger
+battery
+original memory card

From: redfacedass
To: pete j

Dear Peter,

I've been having a rough time at home, so I decided to get away and visit my long lost aunty in Macclesfield. On the way back from her place, I stopped off in rather nice pub called 'The Dolphin' on Windmill Street (are you familiar with it?). I was in need of something to steady my nerves as my aunty has become quite ill. One pint of ale soon led to another and then onto a rather nice brandy. Truth told- I soon felt quite boozie-woozie indeed!

I left the pub, but that wasn't the only thing I left, my jacket I did leave, and along with my jacket- my mobile phone, an iPhone 6.

When I came back to get my jacket the phone wasn't there! Peter, do you know anything about this?

Regards

Fredrick Facedass

From: pete j
To: redfacedass

Hi,

Why would I know anything about your phone being stolen? If it's been stolen then firstly it shouldn't have been left unattended or secondly should have been reported to the police.

If your suggesting the phone I'm selling is yours how the hell would I have nicked your charger, handsfree kit, box etc too and also I have a genuine receipt for when I bought it with the IMEI number on it???

You really need to have a think about what you are writing before you send it, look at my feedback- do I look like a dodgy person that goes around nicking mobile phones?

Regards Pete

From: redfacedass
To: pete j

Dear Peter,

Firstly, you are of course right, I should never have left my phone unattended. I was squiffy at the time; hence my judgment wasn't at its best. Secondly- I did report this theft to the police who, to no surprise, were rather unhelpful. They did however point me in the direction of these shops that specialise in selling stolen goods, like 'Cash Convertors' for example. I tried looking in these stolen goods shops to no avail, and decided to widen the 'net' as it were to eBay, at which point I came across you.

In answer to your question about how you had managed to get hold of my hands-free kit, charger, box, receipt etc? It really would have been rather easy for you, as all of these items were kept with my phone in my jacket.

You are right though Peter, I have looked closely at your very impressive feedback and some of the things you have bought (I liked the trousers you purchased in Sept by the way), and I MUST admit, you do not seem like a dodgy person at all.

So, Peter just to eliminate you from my search once and for all, may I ask you one question-are you blonde?

Kindest Regards
Fredrick Facedass

From: pete j
To: redfacedass

You carry a phone, charger, box and receipt in your jacket? Do you have some XXXL size jacket then?

If your phone is stolen get a crime ref number from the police and claim on your insurance, if you're not insured then it's your loss on this occasion.

What would hair colour have to do with your search for a mobile phone?

Regards Pete

From: redfacedass
To: pete j

My dearest Peter,

Yes! I do indeed carry those items in my jacket. I wear a rather large shooting jacket which can hold many things; including a hip flask, diary, address book, calendar, compass, AAA road atlas, a phone book (which I was told by some big shot was useless as the numbers could be easily stored on a mobile phone. Luckily I ignored this advice as it has proved most useful ever since the crime in question), Nik Naks and seedless grapes (I hate seeded grapes). Think you will agree that it is quite the coat!

I am not insured. Insurance is by-product of pessimism.

A polish barmaid in 'The Dolphin', her name I forget, but whose mammaries will hold heavy in my mind forever, saw a young man with blonde hair leave the pub most abruptly. This man bought nothing and was seen near my coat at precisely the moment we believe the theft to have taken place. This is why I need to know the colour of your hair in order to eliminate you from my future investigations.

Kindest Regards

Fredrick Facedass

From: redfacedass
To: pete j

Peter,

I don't think you fully understand the severity of the situation at hand. A mobile phone has been stolen.

I will stop at nothing until I have successfully recovered my phone, therefore I must follow any leads I have until their path runs dry. Unfortunately for yourself, the path upon which you stand is completely sodden.

I see you got your buyer, a 'Mr John John 1234' with the winning bid of £54 (congrats on this windfall, btw) I have analysed his recent purchases and very interestingly he seems to have bought a different phone only last week, this leads me to believe that he is a phone dealer of some description, perhaps specialising in phones of the stolen variety?

My next port of call is to contact 'Mr John John 1234' to see if he can shed any light on the situation. That is unless you can confirm (I will require a photo) that you are not a blonde man or you can provide me with a suitable alibi for the 17th May between 4.27pm and 4.31pm, when this atrocity took place.

I look forward to your very swift response

Fredrick Facedass

From: pete j
To: redfacedass

You really are messed up in the head I did NOT steal your phone! I was at work on the 17th May at the time stated in Macclesfield. No I am not blonde in hair colour.

Here is a copy of my emailed receipt:

This email confirms the order you have placed online. REF NO.- MF818289
1x sim free mobile phone- iPhone 6 @269.95 GBP
Shipping method: Royal Mail Special Delivery. Shipping cost £5.00 GBP Total: 274.95 GBP

*To track the status of your order you can login to *******.co.uk*
*Thank you for shopping at *******.co.uk*

I bought this phone NEW on *******.co.uk Please DO contact them with my reference number to check I did buy it from them if you don't believe me.

Thanks Peter

Check Material - Unwanted Gift

Q Enlarge

Current bid **£0.60**

Enter maximum bid:

Place bid

Seller info

jkl114 (200 ★)

100% Positive Feedback

Item location: Portsmouth

BRAND NEW - UNWANTED GIFT

beige, black, red, white check material

length 60 inches Width 60 inches

Make a lovely winter skirt etc.
Will not be relisted again on eBay

From: redfacedass
To: jkl114

Dear Jkl,

Happy Birthday!! Hope you had a great time.

I'm sorry to hear you didn't like your present, but I can see why! Material isn't really a gift. A jumper (for example) would be a good gift. But for someone to say *"Oh here's some material go and make yourself something nice"*- They have just given you some extra work to do, haven't they?

Did they also give you some eggs, flour, sugar and milk and tell you to go and bake yourself a cake?!

Well hope you had a good birthday (despite the poor gift)…

Warmest regards,
Fredrick Facedass

From: jkl114
To: redfacedass

Actually for your information I had just started up dressmaking.

If you haven't got anything to do but be very Rude you must lead a very dull life or maybe try bidding for one on E-bAY. ha ha

From: redfacedass
To: jkl114

Dear Jkl,

I'm sorry it was never my intention to be rude. I'm not quite myself at the moment and I have been told before that sometimes my turn of phrase can be inappropriate or even rude, but I just don't realise when I'm doing it!

Isn't it rude to sell a gift?

I do have plenty of things to do. I choose to do this.

Can I please still buy the material from you? Would £6.00 cover the cost and postage?

Warm Regards
Fredrick Facedass

From: jkl114
To: redfacedass

Sorry it has been sold

MacGregor & MacDuff 8 yard 100% Wool Kilt 34-36"

Current bid **£37.00**

Enter maximum bid: | Place bid

Seller info

steviecree (1824) | Item location: Glasgow
100% Positive Feedback

MacGregor and MacDuff full 8 yard 100% wool kilt
Tartan: CAMPBELL OF ARGYLL
This has been lightly used, weddings and special occasions
The kilt is in excellent condition
Measures:
Waist 34" - 36"
Length 25"
Weight: approx 1.3 Kilo
A real heavy weight 100% wool kilt

the price online is approx £300
I need to replace this as I have outgrown it (my good feeding)

From: redfacedass
To: steviecree

Dear Stevie Cree,

Sadly my aunty has just passed away (when I recently visited her she really did seem to be in a lot of distress, so I suppose it's for the best).

The funeral is coming up and the old lady went a bit (a lot) senile in her old age and made drastic changes to her will, mostly benefiting my bank balance ;)

One very strange amendment she made to her will was that she wanted a traditional Scottish funeral and everyone to dress appropriately. Our family is Greek Cypriot with absolutely no connection to the Scots whatsoever, so I'm sure you will appreciate this is a strange decision?

In two weeks' time there will be about 40 Cypriot men all dressed in kilts at a funeral in Macclesfield! (What a funny world we all live in now!)

Just wondering, is kilt Gaylic for skirt?

I'm hoping I will never have to wear a skirt again, so I tried to buy some checked material to bodge up my own kilt (skirt) to save me a little cash, but unfortunately missed out on that one, so now I will have to splash out on a proper skirt :(

Growing up in Cyprus and then in East London, if I had worn a skirt before now, I probably would have been murdered! (Cyprus was rather homophobic whilst I grew up though).

Why do the Scots wear skirts??

Can I wear a belt with this particular skirt you're selling? Sometimes I take a 34 or 36-inch waist and I certainly don't want this falling down (or up if I were upside down!).

Is the colour suitable for a funeral?

Warm regards Fredrick

From: steviecree
To: redfacedass

Hello Fredrick,

I do take great offence of the amount of times you have called our "National Dress" a skirt!

You perhaps should have done your research before contacting me. Kilt is Gaelic for bed! Maybe watch Braveheart for this one?

You mentioned Homophobic... be assured if you ever stated anything in this vain to a Scotsman you would end up hospital. We are a very proud nation!

You do wear a belt, a sporn, a shirt, a jacket, brogue shoes and wool socks... again before you decide to bid do your research. I suggest that you put in your eBay search bar full dress kilt - this will give you a fair idea. Also due to the belts at the side the Kilt goes from a size 34 - a size 36

From: redfacedass
To: steviecree

Dear Stevie,

I am terribly sorry to have caused offence. You are right I should perhaps have done my own research before contacting yourself. I am a little old fashioned, in that I prefer to get my facts and figures from an actual person, rather than the computer (I don't trust computers), hope you understand...

However following your suggestion, I have done a little computer-based research:

Firstly, I have taken note that you prefer people to refer to the kilt as a 'Dress', rather than a 'Skirt' (I will try not to use this word again out of respect for you).

It seems Scotsmen started wearing dresses in the late 16th century; at this point in time it was a full body item with a cloaked top which could be worn over the head or fell loosely around the shoulders. By the late 17th century the top part of the dress had gone leaving only the bottom half of the dress (referred to in other countries as a skirt (sorry)).

It seems the Scotsmen have decided to keep the traditional title of 'Dress' or 'National Dress' despite the drastic alterations in the garment over time, which we should respect. Please do correct me if I am wrong, after all this did come from a computer?

I took on board your suggestion to watch Braveheart to investigate 'kilt' being Gaelic for bed, but found nothing? I did, however, find out that Braveheart has many factual inaccuracies- a major one being the term 'Braveheart'. This was never actually applied to 'William Wallace' (lead character in the film), it was used for 'Robert the Bruce'?! On top of that the movie portrays 'Wallace' and his largely lowland Scotsmen as wearing kilts/dresses, whereas lowlanders did not wear dresses at that time! I have therefore decided to dismiss Braveheart from our research into your national dresses. Hope you understand why I HAD to make that decision.

I did also look up the dictionary definition of kilt too, but I fear you will not like it!

Kilt n.
A knee-length skirt (sorry*) with deep pleats, usually of a tartan wool, worn as part of the dress for men in the Scottish Highlands.

A skirt (sorry*) worn by women, girls, and boys.

* 'sorry' wasn't in the dictionary (I added it to appease you)

You say that your nation is proud to be homophobic- I do think that is a little sad in this day and age, that a whole nation can feel this way. It is a little ironic though that the Scots are the ones wearing dresses!

Well it has been nice chatting with you and look forward to hearing from you soon,

Fredrick

From: steviecree
To: redfacedass

Please STOP sending emails

MY WELL WORN TIGHTS
PRIVATE SALE! ***

Current bid **£2.25**

Enter maximum bid: [   ] **Place bid**

Seller info

supersexylonglegs (14)

100% Positive Feedback

Item location: Bathroom Floor

SEXY BLACK never WORN TIGHTS!
HERE YOU GO BOYS!
You've been asking for it-now its here..
MY SEXY BLACK TIGHTS!
Bid hard and fast just the way I like it!

Make sure you email me and tell me
how much you enjoyed my tights
and any questions at all :) xxx

From: redfacedass
To: supersexylonglegs

Dear Super Sexy Long Legs,

I was wondering if you could do me a 'job lot' of used tights, underwear, socks and any other bits and bobs you may have lying around that you don't need anymore. They really can be in very used condition (in fact the more used the better!) I don't want brand new stuff, as that would be a bit wasteful.

I'm sure I could give you a good price for them…

So let me know exactly what you have got and we can talk £££'s

Many Thanks
Fredrick

From: supersexylonglegs
To: redfacedass

Hi Hun,

You tell me exactly what you want and how many of each and I can sort you out a price. Let me know if you want g-strings or full backed panties or maybe both styles.

All my panties are worn for 24 hours and can be just as wet as you like. Let me know if you want me to play with myself whilst wearing them…. I'll be really happy to oblige, as I love the thought of men getting enjoyment and pleasure out of my used things…

Jennifer xxx

From: redfacedass
To: supersexylonglegs

Hi Jennifer,

Well, I want as much as you can spare that you don't need anymore. No fishnets though as they always get stuck in the teeth!!

You give me a list and name the price.

Play what with yourself? Solitaire?

Many thanks Fredrick

From: supersexylonglegs
To: redfacedass

Hi Fredrick

How about the following-

5 pairs of panties (mainly g strings) that are quite old and worn, and I will make sure I wear each pair and forget to wash them.

3 pairs of natural coloured tights also worn

3 pairs of socks worn and forgotten to wash

3 pairs of pop socks worn and forgotten to wash

Would that do for now?

Altogether that's 14 items (20 if you count the socks and pop socks separately). So, I think a total of £30 and free first class postage…

Let me know what you think Hun and if there is anything else you want?

Jennifer xxx

From: redfacedass
To: supersexylonglegs

Oh my Jennifer you are forgetful! I too used to be forgetful until I found 'cornishwitch' on eBay- sounds crazy but she cast a spell, which really helped me out a lot (check her out, it really is £10 well spent)

I think you must have forgotten that the things you are selling were 'used' when you priced up this bundle?

I could get that lot new for the price you are asking! A simple mistake on your behalf I'm sure!

Please get back to me with the corrected price.

Many thanks,
Fredrick

From: supersexylonglegs
To: redfacedass

LOL What can I say, I am a scatty girlie! I must look into taking a trip to the launderette at some point...

Why don't you offer me a price, bearing in mind I will have to buy myself some new panties socks and tights, it is getting a bit nippy for not wearing any panties

I have already saved the panties I was wearing yesterday in case you want them

Jennifer xxx

From: redfacedass
To: supersexylonglegs

Hi Jennifer,

I think perhaps we have got our wires crossed here.

It seems you are expecting to sell this used underwear for more than the price it costs to get new stuff?!

Why on earth would people pay more for used underwear?

I am after a job lot of unwanted used underwear. Perhaps I should explain my situation; my Jack Russell- Stephen is ludicrously particular about where he goes to the toilet (he only goes on our rug or our sofa). NOT ONCE HAS HE DEFECATED IN THE GARDEN. That was at least until we discovered the mesmerising effect of tights and other female laundry (not fish nets they get stuck in his teeth!) He is so hooked on playing with tights and underwear, that if we keep enough of them strewn across our lawn he stays outside and forgets his old toiletry habits. I can't explain what an enormous relief this was for my wife Talia and I. Trust me there is more than enough of a strain on our relationship at the moment :(

The problem we now face is that we can't supply Stephen's demand. Every day he wants more More MORE…

Talia ran out of underwear to give him a week ago now and we have been buying him new underwear ever since. This seems ridiculous. Firstly it doesn't make sense to spend all that money. Secondly it's bad for the environment.

That's why I decided to buy bulk second hand underwear to try and keep the pup (and my bank balance) happy.

I just can't win though as now you are telling me it's more expensive and on top of that you will be buying replacement underwear! So it's actually even worse than buying it brand-new!!!

Kind regards Fredrick

From: supersexylonglegs
To: redfacedass

Yeah whatever!! Jennifer xxx

PLEASE HELP ME PAY MY STUDENT DEBT

Current bid   **£0.00**

Enter maximum bid: _____   Place bid

Seller info

toffee (0 ⚫)
0% Positive Feedback

Item location: Bristol

Buy my student debt and I will send you a personal thank you for the amount you give me.

A little but about me:

I completed my degree last year and have been struggling to pay off my debt and I need help. I work very hard and would eventually like to start up my own business, but I need money to get rid of the debt from my student days. I can't see my paying if off for years. How will I ever be able to afford to start a family or buy a property when all my earnings go on my bills and debt???

+++++++PLEASE PLEASE PLEASE HELP ME++++++++

From: redfacedass
To: toffee

Toffee,

How's it going? I'm good thanks.

A recent inheritance from my late aunty has left me VERY wealthy and I'm looking for ways to make good use of this wealth. I feel I must ask you this- are you begging?

Regards Fredrick

From: toffee
To: redfacedass

I suppose in a way, yes. I am not standing on the street begging but using today's technology to appeal for help with a genuine debt.

From: redfacedass
To: toffee

Dear Toffee,

As far as I am aware you are not the only person in debt. You've got a degree, why don't you get a job?

Regards Fredrick

From: toffee
To: redfacedass

I do have a job. I am paying my debt and will continue to do so if no one helps. I owe a lot of money and it is depressing when there is no end in sight. I have decided to be proactive and find ways of decreasing it. My ad on eBay is just one of these. I have signed up for a few quiz shows and have a few other things in the pipeline.

I also know too well that other people are in debt. They can also use the Internet to appeal for help like I have if they choose to. Many friends of mine are in debt and they are also finding it difficult and only a few of them are students.

I was spurred on to do this because I saw adverts for people who are about to start university. They are appealing for help before they have any debt (there are a few on eBay at the moment). Well, I am there, I have the debt and I am up to my eyeballs! Am I not allowed to ask for help as well?

I do have over 20K in student loans. If you are interested in helping, then please help. However, if you are simply trying to make me feel bad for putting an ad on eBay then please think again. I am not committing a crime, and I am not a bad person. I would never steal to pay off my debt, sell drugs or sell my body. I was just hoping that placing this ad would cause someone out there to understand and help me.

P.S By questioning me you have already made me feel like a bad person for doing this. So if that is what you intended then you have succeeded

From: redfacedass

To: toffee

Dearest Toffee,

I think you have misunderstood me, as it was never my intention to make you feel bad :(

I have thought very carefully about what you have said in your previous messages…

Now then, let me pose you another question- if you could wipe your debt clean by either-

Furthering your own career
OR
Receiving a donation from a mysterious benefactor

Which would you choose??

Kindest Regards
Fredrick

From: toffee
To: redfacedass

I would further my career without a doubt. I want to be successful, I am very ambitious and I am determined to eventually own a business. I am slowly climbing the ladder but it takes time and I cannot pursue my own business plans because I do not have the money. It all goes on my debt and I am reluctant to add to it with a business loan.

I want to clear my debts, so I can start a fresh life. I suppose I feel like I have not moved on from my student days because I am still carrying around the baggage. You could compare it to breaking up with someone. In order to be completely free, you remove their objects, put their picture away and look to the future. A cleansing process. This is what I want to do with the debt I am carrying around.

However, I question whether I would be happy for a mystery person to clear my debt. I would not have the sense accomplishment if someone cleared it for me, but I don't see myself clearing it any time soon. It's a double-edged sword. I won't know how I feel until it happens. I feel guilty whenever someone shows interest in paying it off. The only reason I keep the advert on there is because I know in my heart of hearts that any money someone offered to pay would definitely go on my debt. I am too much of a worrier and would feel incredibly guilty if I did anything otherwise.

I think I went slightly wayward with my answer. Just to clarify; I would further my career if someone offered me the choice of the two.

From: redfacedass
To: toffee

You see my friend.............even beggars CAN be choosers.

VAGINA TIGHTENING CREAM
Satisfy your man - increase your own pleasure

Quantity: **99 available**

Price: **£9.99** Buy it now

Seller info

lusciousrose (136 ⚹) Item location: Malaysia

100% Positive Feedback

**'Manjakani' has helped countless couples enjoy fulfilling sex again and rekindle their passion for one another.
It has been known to improve relationships in and out of the bed!**

What's in it?
It contains extract of oak galls, a natural ingredient that increases muscle tension in the lower vagina, enabling a firmer grip for increased sexual enjoyment.

How to I use it?
Squeeze a little Manjakani cream onto your finger and sweep within the vagina. The effect is almost immediate

From: redfacedass
To: lusciousrose

Dear Luscious Rose,

The wife and I have been having a VERY tough time, but since my recent inheritance, she has decided we should make a real go of things. With our newfound wealth we have been able to enjoy some of the finer things in life, like seedless grapes (I hate seeded grapes) whenever we feel like it! We do still have one big problem though…

I shall explain- Talia has been, until recently, enjoying a very active sex life with her (leathery-dog-faced internet) friends behind my back. As I'm sure you can imagine this has had a rather negative effect on Talia's nether regions and our relationship. The relationship, as you know, we are working on. It's her nether regions we need your assistance with…

Truth be told, her front entrance is in a terrible condition.

Through a conker contest I stumbled across the amazing tightening/hardening effects of vinegar. We have been trying to utilise this discovery to rekindle our love life. I have found by dipping my wife's vagina in a bucket of vinegar (not brown malt vinegar) for half an hour each morning that she becomes noticeably tighter. This has been a great help in resurrecting our faltering love life, I can assure you.

The only problem is the vinegar seems to have tainted the colour of the skin as well as having a detrimental effect on the smell and taste.

We have just seen your product and are interested, having never seen anything like this!

Are you selling vinegar?

Does your product have any sort of effect on the colour or taste of the vagina? Look forward to hearing from you soon.

Warm regards,
Fredrick Facedass

From: lusciousrose
To: redfacedass

Hi Fredrick,

I never heard something like this but it's ok because I received funny- funny question from all over the world about this product.

Yes I sell vinegar, but apple cider vinegar, but that product is for cooking and losing weight. How to take good care of a woman intimate area? This is what I do, I cleanse and moisturize it.

Do not use normal soap to wash it, search for feminine hygiene that is ph3.5, this will prevent discolouration and the smell? Each time after sex, no matter how tired she is, she still have to go to bathroom and wash it, make sure cleanse everything properly with a proper soap and towel dry. If the smell is still around insert a small amount of manjakani cream insert the vagina. This product will leave a very pleasant smell on the vagina but if the smell continues to be there. Please asked her to go to the doctor and make sure she finish her anti-biotic

Use Allano moisturiser from Anway to moisturise her private part. Follow my advice and she will have a ***** just like Tara Patrick ;)

Cheers,
Luscious Rose

From: redfacedass
To: lusciousrose

Dear Luscious Rose,

I recently purchased some 'Manjakani Plus Gel' for my wife Talia's damaged vagina. You also issued us with some advice that has proved to be disastrous. If you recall, I mentioned that we had successfully experimented with vinegar, so we were very intrigued at your suggestion to try apple cider vinegar.

The cider vinegar did have an excellent tightening effect, however, it also had a nasty reaction with the skin- making it very itchy, dry, flaky, and really rather sore (Talia has been immobilised for the last two days, due to the incredible pain). We also followed your advice and used the 'Manjakani Plus Gel' to try and eliminate the smell, with limited success.

We are not looking for a refund, but we just thought we really ought to let you know about this, in case you had passed on this TERRIBLE advice to any of your other customers.

Regards Fredrick

From: lusciousrose

To: redfacedass

Hi Fred

You make me laughed;) I did not asked you to dip in apple cider vinegar, I said I sell apple cider vinegar, and that stuff is for cooking and dieting

I still have that email that I send you Fred, no advise on dipping in apple cider vinegar.

Please STOP asking your wife to dip in vinegar, it's not healthy Fred.

Don't worry I will not advise anybody to dip in vinegar ;)

'cheers'
Nina

UNDATED 20p COIN - ROYAL MINT ERROR- VERY RARE AND VERY VALUABLE

Price: £3,250,000.00   **Buy it now**

Best offer: **Make offer**

Seller info

great-UK-items   (14)   Item location: Wigan

100% Positive Feedback

This coin is EXTREMELY RARE due to an error at The Royal Mint the coins were minted without a date on either side as you may know there are not that many of these coins left, and as the days go on these coins are getting even more rare!

It is over 350 years since a British coin has been minted without a date.
No more will be circulated.
This is your only chance.

1 coin has already sold eBay for £1.7m and the value is only forecast to increase.

HERE IS YOUR CHANCE TO INVEST!!

From: redfacedass
To: great-UK-items

Dear Great,

I have recently inherited a LOT of money from my late aunty.

I am looping for various ways to invest this. I could see this as an investment.

It would have to be a lot less though. What would you go to?

Regards
Fred

From: great-UK-items
To: redfacedass

Hi there sir.

Thanks for your message. Sir how much would you like to give me? Let me know. Cheers

From: redfacedass
To: great-UK-items

Sir,

Well face value is 20 so that is how much I would give to you. How much do want me to give you?

Regards
Fred

From: great-UK-items
To: redfacedass

No mate. THE PRICE THAT YOU HAVE GIVEN ME IS TOTALLY UNACCEPTABLE. I HAVE HAD OFFERS OF 250,000 POUNDS. THE PRICE I AM LOOKING FOR IS MINIMUM 500K.

From: redfacedass
To: great-UK-items

Hi Sir,

Just sounding you out.

That's a shame though because I had 200k in mind and you obviously won't go for that!!!!!

Cheers all the same- Fred

From: great-UK-items
To: redfacedass

WELL, I HAVE TALKED TO MY DAD AND HE GOES TO ME THAT ITS OKAY FOR 200K. LET ME

KNOW BACK IF YOU WANT IT CHEERS. IF YOU DONT WANT IT THEN I WILL GIVE IT TO ANOTHER BUYER WHO IS GIVING THE SAME. JUST POP A OFFER ON MY ITEM AND I WILL ACCEPT IT.

CHEERS

From: redfacedass
To: great-UK-items

Sir,

Who's in charge of this sale- you or your dad?

I am a little confused. In your last message you stated that you had more than one offer for

£250,000. I have just offered you 200k, which is obviously MUCH less than the offers you already have…

How's your maths? Only robbing a young boy on eBay won't mape me feel all that good, and as far as I am aware you don't owe me any favours? And certainly not thousands of them!!

Check out your figures with your old man, and send another message to me if you are still interested though.

All the best Fred

From: great-UK-items
To: redfacedass

Hi there. Sorry about that. Its okay, I will accept 200k. Cheers, very sorry about that.

From: redfacedass
To: great-UK-items

Sir,

Why are you akologising?

Also, you haven't answered any of the questions from my last message.

Again- why won't you take the offers for £250,000? It does leave this whole deal seeming a little fishy.

Seriously, I am struggling to talp business with you. How old are you? You should get your old man on- so I can get some straight answers.

Fred

From: great-UK-items
To: redfacedass

Hi there. Well you can call me on 07888 65**** sir I am genuine, just call me. Cheers

From: redfacedass
To: great-UK-items

Sir,

Just made my offer for 200k (Fingers crossed!!)

Fred

From: great-UK-items
To: redfacedass

SIR YOU HAVE PUT 2.00 POUNDS

From: redfacedass
To: great-UK-items

Sir,

Yes that's right £2, which is 200k. Ten times the value of the coin! Is there a kroblem?

Regards Fred

From: great-UK-items
To: redfacedass

No you think I'm a fool. 2.00 is not the same as 200k.

From: redfacedass
To: great-UK-items

Sir,

There must be some confusion! My offer is for 200 kence!

Just realised the letters on my peyboard have worn off I must have stucp the letters the wrong way round for the k and the p. No way would I kay £200,000 for a 20k coin!!

(My offer still stands though- and it is the current highest offer?)

Pind Regards

Fredricp Facedass

From: great-UK-items
To: redfacedass

A TOTAL TIME WASTER, AND A JOKER. YOU HAVE MESSED ME ABOUT AND CERTAINLY A REDASS. CHEAP SHIT. IF YOU CANT PAY THEN WHY BOTHER EMAILING..........WASTE SOMEONE ELSE TIME IF U WASTE MINE AGAIN, THEN WILL GET POLICE INVOLVED. AND NO YOUR OFFER IS NOT THE HIGHEST, LIKE I SAID BEFORE I HAVE COSTUMERS,
NOT CHEAP IDIOTS LIKE U...................

From: redfacedass
To: great-UK-items

Sir,

By the way, I just thought I should let you pnow that you might have same peyboard kroblem as me only with the letters 'O' and 'U'.

See "costumers" in your last message; thinp you meant to write 'customers'. (Unless of course you meant- "One that mapes or sukklies costumes" in which case I stand corrected!)

Good lucp with the sale and all the best Fred

From: great-UK-items
To: redfacedass

SHUT UP AND DO ONE.......... THICK SHIT

Hewlett Packard Keyboard

Current bid **£0.00**

Enter maximum bid: Place bid

Seller info

retabe (342 ⚖)   Item location: Birmingham

100% Positive Feedback

🔍 Enlarge

for sale
hewlett packard keyboard
hardly used
boxed
cost £20
I'll start at 10p
pnp will be £5

From: redfacedass
To: retabe

Dear Retabe,

I am having a few kroblems with my KC peyboard at the moment and I am in the marpet for a suitable reklacement.

Can you still see the letters on the peys clearly, or are they pnacpered like mine?

Can you believe my faulty peyboard has had me threatened with kolice action!

Pind regards,
Fredricp Facedass

From: retabe
To: redfacedass

Using it now, works gucking freat!!

The Killing of John Lennon DVD

Enlarge

Current bid **£1.00**

Enter maximum bid:

Place bid

Seller info

lovebeetle (221)
100% Positive Feedback

Item location: Rhonnda

The killing of John Lennon DVD.

Brand new and sealed.
U.K postage £2.00

121

From: redfacedass
To: lovebeetle

Hi there!

Can you message me the blurb on the back please?

Thanks in advance,
Fredrick Facedass

From: lovebeetle
To: redfacedass

the killing of John Lennon is a chilling insight into the mind of mark David Chapman the 25 year old who gunned down John Lennon outside his Dakota apartment in new york in 1980 meticulous researched and filmed on actual location where events occurred, it is a gritty and imagistic examinattion of a celebrity stalkers mind leading up to the kill and a look into his descent into madness and exorcism.independently financed and filmed over three years, the killing of john lennon is unflinching in its presentation of the truth.

hope this helps regards,

Shelia

From: redfacedass
To: lovebeetle

Thanks for the quick response.

As I suspected it says exactly the same on the back of my copy too!

Regards,
Fredrick Facedass

From: lovebeetle
To: redfacedass

Nice one! Regards Shelia

From: redfacedass
To: lovebeetle

No problem Shelia,

What year was yours made? And who directed your copy?
Regards Fredrick

From: lovebeetle
To: redfacedass

Year 2006, by Andrew Piddington. Regards Shelia

LOVE & ROMANCE, HYPNOSIS CD

Price: **$7.99**   Buy it now

Best offer: _____   Make offer

Seller info
patriciolove (347)   Item location: Kansas
100% Positive Feedback

Open your heart, Heal the past and realise your highest potential this meditation/ hypnosis CD is designed for opening your heart to deeper levels of Loves potential and higher levels of Blissful Romantic energy.

Healing and letting go of the past and creating a present moment of higher love and Higher Romance for an incredibly full and passionate future...

Realising yourself as all Love and all that can be...

From: redfacedass
To: patriciolove

Hello Patricio Love,

Is that your real name? (I really hope so!!)

I have been having a bit of rough time with my wife. We've tried to make a go of things recently, but it's simply not working. So, we've separated again- I'm back down in the basement, whilst Talia is up in the main house with Stephen (our dog).

She has had many group indiscretions behind my back, I forgave her for these, but still she doesn't want me back. I have been a loving caring husband and it hurts that she doesn't want me.

Patricio- I'm desperate to get her back and I am thinking of paying a witch on eBay to cast a permanent spell on her to MAKE her love me (I've successfully used an eBay witch before, btw).

But, I think I have a better idea! After doing some computer-based research I have come to learn that hypnosis can work on people whilst they are asleep? Please confirm this is so.

What I'm thinking (with your help) is that whilst she is sleeping, I could sneak up into the main house, armed with a small music player, and hypnotise her into loving me again.

Will this work? Are you in?

Regards Fred

From: patriciolove
To: redfacedass

You need to do this work to get her back from your heart, not though fake witches and sneaking around. Perhaps this kind of pattern is one of the reasons she wants you away from her.....

I can't help you. But good luck, with your heart work, no matter what happens.

Alaya, for Patricio Love

From: redfacedass
To: patriciolove

Hello Patricio,

Is your name really Patricio Love?

Fake witches? No really there are some witches on eBay who can help with all sorts, trust me I speak with first-hand experience.

I have been thinking about your comments regarding my sneakiness and the work I need to do on my heart and have decided that your CD could actually be of benefit to me. The only thing is, I have this strange condition where I can't listen to anything from a music player of any sort whilst awake; it makes me irritable, irrational and sometimes terribly sad. I LOVE listening to music whilst I am asleep though...

I was thinking that I could pop the CD player on a timer to play whilst I am in deep sleep. Would listening to this CD work whilst I am sleeping?

Look forward to hearing from you soon.

Alaya (what does Alaya mean, btw?)

Fred

From: patriciolove
To: redfacedass

The CDs are made to listen to while fully awake. They would not work as well at all listening to them while deep asleep. Sorry about that..

From: redfacedass
To: patriciolove

Hi Patricio,

Might it work a little?
Is your name really Patricio Love?

Many thanks,
Fred

From: patriciolove
To: redfacedass

Like I mentioned, it is not recommended to listen to these CDs while asleep. I can't honestly say it will help you, or either of you while sleeping. Perhaps someone else has what you need. Something more subliminal, that might work if you listen to it all night long for months…

**From: redfacedass
To: patriciolove**

Hi Patricio,

Is your name really Patricio Love?

How you doing? It's been a while. I have been living life like a fox ((nocturnally) not eating out of bins!!!!)

I decided to follow your advice and I bought a more powerful subliminal hypnosis CD from another eBay seller.

I realised that the chimney from the house runs down into the basement, so whilst Talia was out I hid some tiny little speakers in the fireplace in her (our) room and ran wires down the chimney down to the basement (my current home).

Needless to say for the last 5 weeks Talia has been listening to *'Love and Abundance'* from midnight till 7am EVERY single day. A baby monitor installed under her bed lets me to know when she is asleep. Unfortunately it also lets me know when her leathery dog-faced friends are round too. Not a nice listen I can assure you :(

It's been strange keeping these new hours, but hopefully it will be worth it! I would do anything to get her back. She's so wonderful. However, currently this doesn't seem to be working, as I haven't seen her for absolutely ages now. I guess we are just keeping such different hours at the moment? But persist I must.

Alaya, Fred

From: patriciolove
To: redfacedass

I will NOT be responding to your questioning anymore.

Alaya, for Patricio Love

From: redfacedass
To: patriciolove

Hey Patricio,

Is your name really Patricio Love?

What does Alaya mean?

Alaya, Fred

LAST MINUTE YURT BREAK

⊕ Enlarge

Current bid **£170**

Enter maximum bid: [ ] **Place bid**

Seller info

gillandtimothy (87)   Item location: Devon

100% Positive Feedback

Last minute YURT, TIPI holiday in North Devon
From 2pm fiday 10th August till 10 am on monday 13th August

The best and most comfy yurts in North Devon.
Come and relax around a camp fire.... on site
there are two fishing lakes, licensed cafe, play area,
farm shop. These Holidays normally sell at £350 so be quick...

From: redfacedass
To: gillandtimothy

Dear Gillandtimothy,

I've been having a bad time recently and after reading your advert- I've decided to treat myself to a peaceful weekend away, but at the same time not *too* peaceful. I feel like I MUSN'T be alone (my doctor agrees too).

Would you (and/or your staff) be able to not only accommodate me, but also accompany me during my stay? I am a very easy and fun person to be around and I won't be any trouble for you (or your staff).

I will be making daily excursions to visit the local area, I liked the look of Coarse Fishing, so I thought perhaps we (you (or one of your staff) and I) could go there? What do you say- could be quite fun?!

I understand a new price will reflect my extra requirements. What kind of price are you thinking? Really looking forward to getting away from it all and just generally chilling out with you.

Best regards Fred

From: gillandtimothy
To: redfacedass

Hi Fred

I don't actually have any staff and as much as I would love to spend the weekend fishing, the Mrs. has so many jobs for me to do she won't let me

Cheers Timothy

From: redfacedass
To: gillandtimothy

My dearest Timothy,

Thanks for your swift response.

I know exactly where you are coming from when it comes to household chores. Trust me, I used to be under my wife's thumb too!

Timothy - I'm sure we would have such a great time fishing and who knows we could turn out to be the best of friends? I'd like that, so let's talk this through...

Seems like the main stumbling block here is your chores? So why don't I just help you out with your work. I've come up with a problem-solving itinerary for our weekend-

FRIDAY
2 PM I arrive, make myself at home, unpack etc

6 PM Freshen up

7 PM Head out to Mario's restaurant- all on me of course. You can bring your wife too (could be a great chance for me to finally meet her)

SATURDAY

7 AM Fishing, bonding and generally chilling out with you.

7 PM BBQ (hopefully we can cook up our catches!!)

SUNDAY
AM   Job day
Nb. this is *your* day, so you will have to come up with the finer details for this.

MONDAY
11AM   I'll be making my way home (refreshed and relaxed)

I'm off to re-fix Beatrice's guttering (the last lot was installed very badly a few months ago and needs mending already). See you Friday.

Kindest regards
Fred

From: gillandtimothy
To: redfacedass

What's your phone number? I will call you. Cheers Timothy

From: gillandtimothy
To: redfacedass

Fred

I still have not agreed to anything so if you do wish for me accompany you for the weekend we need to discuss this and

quickly as the tents are selling fast my mobile number is 0***
****

Cheers Timothy

Ps for all I know this could be a scam and before I agree to spend the weekend with you I would like to know a bit about you how old are you? Where do you live etc if I do not get a phone call from you I will not be selling you a holiday...

From: redfacedass
To: gillandtimothy

Timothy,

I'm sorry for the short notice, but I'm afraid I won't be able to make it this weekend.

Unfortunately, re-fixing Beatrice's gutter hasn't gone as well as I might have hoped. I had a rather nasty fall from her rickety old ladder and I've spent the entire night in A&E with a badly sprained wrist and ankle.

I did try phoning you, but I've been having HUGE trouble making calls from my new phone. I only ever seem to be able to make calls to the emergency services. This turned out to be quite lucky because at the time I was lying in a crumpled heap in Beatrice's garden! I didn't know whom else to call, so that's why I tried to phone you. Trying to call you got me the ambulance that I needed. You saved me Timothy!

Sorry to have let you down at such short notice, but I really won't be much use on that fishing trip that you were so desperate to go on.

I just tried phoning you again, but I think I will have to stop doing that now. The emergency services seem to be getting really annoyed with my incessant calls.

Maybe I should switch my Blackberry over to a phone whose buttons are large enough to accommodate human fingers? (I do miss my old iPhone).

Perhaps when I have fully recovered we can re-schedule another trip? (I think that would be really nice)

Your friend,
Fred

Hi,

I have had a truly terrible year. I shan't bore you with the full details, but I caught my wife cheating on me with internet-friends and our (once happy) relationship is now DEAD.

I thought it would be best to get away from it all and so I had a weekend away planned with my friend Timothy, but unfortunately I had to let Timothy down last minute (I think he's a bit devastated, as he hasn't been in touch since).

I had a brainwave today and have decided that I should travel the world. This is what I need to do. Leave it all behind and clear my head for good.

I would like you to plan me the best trip imaginable. Can you do this? You really can go town here as there is NO real limit to cost.

If you were able to take the time off work- I'd love for you to join me on this trip of a lifetime. I am a fun, easy-going person to be around. All I ask is that you don't snore. I HATE snorers. Will you join me? (I'll pay for everything).

I would love to see all the big sites like The Taj Mahal, The Great Barrier Reef and Luxembourg.

I really am open to suggestions, so where would you like to go? You can add it to the list.

Really looking forward to our adventure together.
Fredrick

From: Suzy*****@***flights.co.uk**
To: redfacedass@*.co.uk**
Subject: Travel Enquiry

Hi Fredrick,

Thank you so much for your online enquiry about the trip you are planning, it sounds like it is going to be amazing!! It's an amazing opportunity for you and sounds like just what you need!

I am very sorry to hear about your wife and the tough time you have been having. It will be great to help you plan this trip, but I do need a little more information from you in order to put together the perfect trip. I did try giving you a call and left you a message, but if you could give me a call back or let me know:

Do you know how long you want to be away for, are you thinking 3,6,9 months or even a year?
Would you like me to look at group tours, that way you will always have a great group of people around you?
Would you like to go to Australia, Antarctica or USA?

If you can let me know a little bit more detail, I look forward to helping you plan this trip.

Regards Suzy

From: redfacedass@*.co.uk**
To: Suzy*****@***flights.co.uk**
Subject: Travel Enquiry

Hi Suzy,

Thank you very much for getting back to me. Firstly- sorry I missed your call, as I mentioned there is very limited reception down in my basement. I called you back, but I guess you wouldn't have been working at 11.30pm? I left a voicemail for you anyway.

I'm SO pleased you will be able to join me on this trip of a lifetime. Thank you! Are you sure it won't be too much trouble for you to take the time of work?

Here are the answers to your questions-

Do you know how long you want to be away for, are you thinking 3, 6,9 months or even a year?

Ideally I'd like to go for a year, but if this were too long for you, then I would consider shortening our trip (let's go for a year!).

Would you like me to look at group tours, that way you will always have a great group of people around you?

Group tours could be a great way of meeting new people. But, I don't deal well with large numbers- anything over 2 is a definite NO.

Would you like to go to Australia, Antarctica or USA?

Would YOU like to go to Australia, Antarctica or USA?

I'll be away most of today, as I am taking an elderly neighbour to get a new hearing aid fitted. So, probably won't be able to take your calls today. Do please email if you can't get through and I can get back to you this evening.

Kind regards Fred

From: Suzy*******@***flights.co.uk
To: redfacedass@***.co.uk
Subject: Travel Enquiry

Hi Fred,

Thank you for getting back to me. I'm sorry to disappoint you, but I won't be able to go with you. Apologies if you read my original email wrong. I've travelled a lot in my years and I can no longer take the time off work to do this anymore. You will have a brilliant time going though and will meet various people on your trip.

If you want to go for a year, that's great as this is the length of most RTW tickets. For First Class you'd be looking at around £15,000 for your flights, and for Business you'd be looking at around £9000. This is based on a fairly standard RTW ticket. How does this sound to you?

Are you able to call me with some payment and then we can plan your trip? We are only open until 6pm, which is the reason I missed your call last night – but thank you for leaving me the voicemail.

Kind Regards,
Suzy

From: redfacedass@*.co.uk**
To: Suzy*****@***flights.co.uk**
Subject: Travel Enquiry

Hi Suzy,

Sorry not to get back to you sooner- Beatrice was very excited that she could finally hear again properly, so I agreed to play a game of Pictionary with her. It went on for rather a long time, hence my late reply!

I shan't push any further, but I am VERY disappointed that you will no longer be coming with me on this trip. Oh well. I guess this is something that I must do by myself. Who knows perhaps it will be good for me to do this on my own...

Thinking about it- I've been down here in this basement for almost six months now and I haven't felt lonely once. In fact (aside from my wife cheating on me with leathery-dog-faced internet friends) it's really been a blast! I've met loads of great people (like you) from my basement, so I'm sure whilst I'm traveling the world I'll meet plenty more.

I'll come into your office to book this trip with you tomorrow morning. I'm really looking forward to finally meeting you. Who knows, when you actually meet me- you may change your mind and come with me? I am VERY handsome ;)

Many thanks Fred

Printed in Great Britain
by Amazon